MW00624326

Introduction

Here at Fall Creek Farm & Nursery, we firmly believe that blueberries are one of Mother Nature's most perfect gifts. Blueberries speak of lazy summer days spent barefoot with a bucket, plucking the deep-colored, juicy orbs of sweetness. Our summer mantra: "One for the bucket, one for me. One for the bucket, one for me…"

Here are just a few of the reasons our family fell deeply, hopelessly in love with blueberries three decades ago:

They taste great and can be eaten from breakfast to dessert.

•

They're nutritious and offer powerful health benefits.

•

They freeze beautifully,
so we can taste a little of summer all year long.

•

They grow on striking plants that add beauty
to our landscape or patio pot.

•

They're versatile landscape plants, suitable for
raised beds, containers and hedges.

•

They're easy to grow, require little care,
and are rarely bothered by pests.

We're such fervent fans of blueberries that we're eager to share the bounty with home gardeners across the country. We hope this little guide will help you discover just how easy it is to cultivate and enjoy one of life's great delights right in your own back yard!

The Brazelton Family

Your Blueberry Toolbox

Here are some helpful tools to help ensure your success in blueberry gardening:

Shovel/spade
•
Supplemental soil for pots and raised beds
•
Soil amendments, including peat moss
•
Acid fertilizer
•
Mulch
•
Sprinklers
•
Bird-proof netting
•
Plant cover in colder regions
•
Pruning tools
•
A knowledgeable,
service-oriented garden center
•
A big bucket for harvesting!

How Many Plants

A common question is "How many plants do I need for my family?" Generally, the average blueberry plant in a home garden will produce 5+ pounds of fruit. Many will produce even more if they're well tended to optimize fruit production.

HERE'S A VERY SIMPLE GUIDE:		
People In Family	Mainly Fresh Eating	Fresh +Baking/Freezing
2	4 plants	8 plants
4	8 plants	16 plants
6	12 plants	24 plants

Blueberry Varieties

While blueberries have earned a very special place in the hearts of berry-lovers around the world, they are so much more than a shrub bearing summer fruit. They're perfect for every season and every garden. They offer beautiful bell-shaped flowers in spring, luscious berries in summer, brilliant foliage in fall and vibrant cane color in winter. Blueberries come in all shapes and sizes from dwarf varieties that stay about 2 feet tall and are suitable for patio pots, to big, tall varieties that are great for hedges.

Because there are so many varieties of blueberries, it's possible to enjoy them in nearly every region of the country. There are selections that produce fruit early, mid and late season, so by planting more than one type, you can extend your blueberry harvest season from early summer through fall. In most regions you can get up to several months of fruit!

There are two primary categories of blueberries – Northern Highbush and Southern Highbush. Widely grown in the northern U.S. and southern Canada, Northern Highbush varieties require colder winters. Southern Highbush varieties do well California, the Sunbelt and the Southeast U.S., where winters are mild. While all blueberry plants have both male and female organs on the same flower, Northern Highbush varieties are self-pollinating, but most Southern Highbush are not. (See page 16 for more information on pollination.)

Your local garden center can help you choose blueberry varieties that do well in your region, including selections to suit your preferences, your taste and your landscape. Blueberries offer endless mix-and-match possibilities. By shopping for specific varieties, you can choose berry textures, sizes, flavors, and ripening times; berries suitable for baking, freezing, or eating fresh; and varieties with dazzling fall color, and specific growth habits.

Check out the tantalizing possibilities on the Blueberry Variety Charts under the Home Gardeners section of our website at www.fallcreeknursery.com.

 DID YOU KNOW THERE ARE MORE THAN 100 BLUEBERRY VARIETIES AVAILABLE? THEY OFFER AN AMAZING ARRAY OF ATTRIBUTES!

Site Selection

Blueberries appreciate a sunny location with well-drained, well-worked soil. Although they relish a spot that gets at least six hours of sun a day, it may be necessary to provide them with partial shade in hotter climates. Also, avoid planting blueberries near a wall in hot climates, since walls absorb and retain heat.

Because blueberries are shallow-rooted, plant them where they don't compete with large rooted trees, shrubs and weeds for water and nutrients. Also, choose a location where irrigation is available, since their roots should be kept moist throughout the growing season.

Soil Preparation

Here's a brief primer on an important component of blueberry gardening: Blueberries like acidic soils. A soil with a pH lower than 7.0 is an acid soil and one with a pH higher than 7.0 is alkaline.

Generally, soils in moist climates tend to be acid and those in dry climates are alkaline.

Some plants require a fairly acidic soil to grow, while others prefer alkaline soil. The pH of the soil greatly affects the availability of nutrients in the soil and is one of the most important factors determining plant growth and overall health. The soil must be adjusted to meet the specific needs of each plant.

Because blueberries prefer acid soil (generally in the 4.5 – 5.5 range), it's important to determine the pH of your soil to grow them successfully. Many garden centers will test a soil sample for pH level for you, or you can buy an inexpensive, easy-to-use pH test kit at most nurseries or hardware stores.

However, there's a shortcut to determining if blueberries will do well in your soil. If you can readily grow azaleas or rhododendrons in your soil, it should be suitable for blueberries, too, since they all prefer the same acidic soil. However, in many regions, it's best to either plant blueberries in a raised bed or a large container to make it easier to amend the soil to proper acidity. Ask your garden center representative to recommend a soil acidifier if necessary for your area.

A failsafe way to grow blueberries in nearly any soil is to incorporate peat moss into the planting medium. Readily available at garden centers, peat moss is the decomposing, dead parts of sphagnum moss that usually are found deep in a bog. It's rich in organic material, and can hold up to 20 times its weight in water. For this reason, peat moss mulch can be used in dry areas to help retain water. It's also acidic and can be used to lower soil pH.

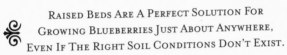

RAISED BEDS ARE A PERFECT SOLUTION FOR
GROWING BLUEBERRIES JUST ABOUT ANYWHERE,
EVEN IF THE RIGHT SOIL CONDITIONS DON'T EXIST.

For planting blueberries directly into the ground, work a planting area approximately 2 feet in diameter and 1 foot deep. Remove one-third to one-half the soil. Add an equal amount of pre-moistened peat moss and mix well. One bale of peat should be plenty for 10 to 20 plants. For raised beds, mix equal volumes peat moss with acid compost or planting mix. As acid-loving plants, blueberries will appreciate coffee grounds, tea bags, wood ash or Epsom salts mixed into the soil as well. Also, watering the soil around plants with a solution of one tablespoon of white vinegar to one gallon of water can also increase soil acidity.

In regions with alkaline or heavy clay soil, blueberries can be grown in containers – the larger, the better. A minimum size is a five-gallon pot. For container plants, buy a planting medium for acid loving plants, or make your own with 50% peat moss, 40% bark mulch and 10% sand.

Planting

Once your soil is properly amended and worked, it's time to plant! Dig a hole larger than needed. Remove the plant from its pot, and lightly roughen up the outside surface of the root ball. Set the top soil line of the pot about one-half inch higher than the existing ground and firm the soil around the root ball. Blueberries can be planted as close as 2 feet apart to form solid hedges or much farther apart for individual specimens.

While fall and spring are typically ideal, in many regions blueberries can be planted just about any time of year. It's a good idea to consult your garden center experts about the optimal time to plant in your area.

Pollination

Blueberry plants produce lots of fruit, but many varieties require bees to do the important work of pollination. Pollen gets stuck to the bees' legs and falls off as they move from plant to plant.

Although all blueberry plants have both male and female organs on the same flower, some varieties are self-pollinating, while others are not. Those that are not self-pollinating must be cross-pollinated with other varieties in order to bear fruit.

 PLANTING MORE THAN ONE BLUEBERRY VARIETY WILL RESULT IN A BETTER FRUIT HARVEST.

The best bet for healthier, more productive blueberries, regardless of type or variety, is to plant different varieties of blueberries within 100 feet of one another, so bees can travel and cross-pollinate the plants. Cross-pollination can result in greater yield, larger fruit, enhanced flavor and better ripening.

Mulching and Fertilizing

Mulching is a simple way to save time and effort later! By spreading 2 to 4 inches of mulch over the roots, you can conserve moisture, prevent weeds, insulate roots from cold temperatures and add vital organic material to the soil. Use bark mulch, acid compost, sawdust or grass clippings, and repeat every other year. Be sure not to mulch with bark or sawdust from cedar or redwood. If you use grass clippings for mulch, be sure to mix with bark, pine needles or straw.

Wait until your blueberry plants are well established before fertilizing them. Once they're established, fertilize them twice a year — once in early spring and again in late spring.

Blueberries like acid fertilizers such as rhododendron or azalea formulations, either granular or liquid. Use according to directions on the label, covering an area roughly the size of a very large dinner plate around the base of the plant.

High-nitrogen organic fertilizers such as blood meal and acidic cottonseed meal work well for blueberries, but avoid cow or chicken manure since it may damage the plant.

Coffee grounds are an inexpensive homemade blueberry fertilizer since they're rich in nitrogen, magnesium and potassium. Plus, they help acidify the soil and make sure your blueberry plants don't get drowsy! Consider occasionally scattering your spent coffee grounds as top dressing around your blueberries.

Watering

Because blueberries have a shallow fibrous root system, they need consistent moisture from the time blossoms appear until fall colors develop and the weather cools. You can either hand water the plants or use a drip, soaker or overhead sprinkler or watering system. The amount of water required varies according to your climate. A general rule of thumb in most areas is to water two or three times a week in summer for blueberries growing directly in the soil or raised beds and every day for containers. Check with your garden center representative for more specific water requirements in your area.

Many dry areas like Arizona, southern California, the Southeast U.S. and Texas have hard water. In these areas, and others where white flaky calcium builds up in showers and faucets, blueberries will perform better if you apply an acidifier to the water occasionally to leach out the calcium that builds up around the roots from irrigation. An easy way to do this is to water twice a week with a vinegar solution. Use 6 ounces of household vinegar per 4 gallons of water and drench around the root ball.

Pruning

Here's perhaps the only difficult aspect of growing blueberries: As painful as it may be, it's important to remove most blooms as they appear in the first year. This allows the plant to become well established and vigorous enough to muster the energy required to produce fruit in subsequent years. (Helpful hint: Most blueberry plants sold in one-gallon pots are one year old. By buying older plants, say those in two- or five-gallon pots, you can avoid removing the blooms and can enjoy fruit the first year after planting!)

 WANT A SIMPLE WAY TO INCREASE
BLUEBERRY FRUIT PRODUCTION IN THE SUMMER?
PRUNE ONCE EVERY WINTER!

After the first year, annual winter pruning is an easy and essential investment into more productive harvests. Pruning older branches that will bear little if any fruit allows the plant to spend its precious energy producing new wood that will bear larger, more abundant berries. Pruning also prevents over-fruiting, which results in small berries or poor plant growth.

See pruning diagrams, next page.

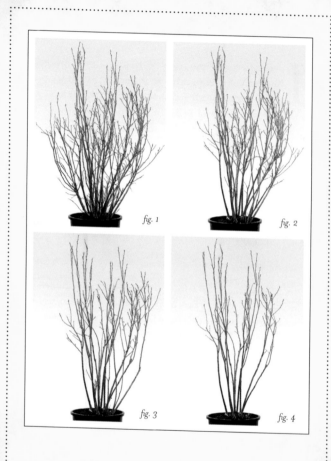

fig. 1

fig. 2

fig. 3

fig. 4

1

After the first year, follow these pruning steps
once the leaves have dropped.

2

Remove low growth around the base.
If it doesn't grow up, it gets pruned out!

3

Remove the dead wood and non-vigorous twiggy wood.
Keep the bright colored wood with long (at least 3 inch)
laterals. Remove blotchy colored short growth.

4

If one-third to one-half of the wood hasn't been removed
by the first two steps, thin out the fruiting laterals and small
branches until this balance has been obtained.

Hand pruners can be used to remove one-year-old wood. If the
wood is two or three years old, a lopper or saw may be used to cut
through the heavier wood.

Pests

Insects aren't generally a problem with blueberries, and most diseases can be easily prevented with careful pruning. Possibly the biggest pests to blueberries aren't really pests at all – they're the birds we work so hard to attract to our gardens. Birds and squirrels love blueberries and can quickly eat an entire crop of unprotected blueberries. You may want to simply plant a few extra bushes just for them! Or, if you're not feeling quite that generous, you may want to invest in improved mesh netting that's now available to deter hungry birds and squirrels from devouring blueberries. Check with your garden center representatives for recommendations.

Cold Protection

Although blueberries are more tolerant of cold weather than other fruits, they're still at risk during a freeze, and are especially sensitive in spring when they're sprouting tender new growth. To protect blueberry plants from frost damage in the winter and early spring, place a plant cover over the tops of the bushes in mid-afternoon on days when freezing temperatures are expected. These covers provide a barrier that helps keep the bushes several degrees warmer. Remove the plant cover once the freeze is over. In regions of extreme cold, it's a good idea to mulch your plants heavily around the base in the winter.

It's also wise to water your blueberry plants more when a freeze is expected. The additional hydration allows the soil to soak up more heat during the day and deliver to the bush for cold protection.

If you live where temperatures may fall below 10°F, it can be a good idea to protect your blueberries in winter. For containers, move them into the garage or mulch to protect the roots. For plantings in raised beds or soil, an additional mulch of leaves around the base will help insulate the roots from the coldest weather.

Blueberries in Containers

Growing blueberries in containers is a snap, and is an attractive option even for those who have abundant garden space. Blueberries in pots can be strategically located on decks, patios or among garden ornamentals to offer year-round color and interest. Growing blueberries in containers also makes it easy to buy or create blueberry-friendly acidic soil.

Dwarf varieties of blueberries are the best long-term choice for containers. Select a well-draining container for your plants at least 20 to 24 inches in size. Wooden half barrels make good blueberry containers. Place the pot where it will remain before adding acidic potting soil and the plant, since the container will be heavy and difficult to move when filled.

If your winters are cold and you're overwintering blueberries in containers, move them against a building or into a protected area like a garage to keep them out of the wind. (Note: Some plant containers have wheels to make them easier to move. Check with your garden center representative for suggestions.) You can also mulch your plants with straw or wrap the containers in burlap to provide additional insulation.

If your containerized blueberry plant outgrows its pot, it can be transplanted during dormancy to a larger container or directly into the garden.

Please note that the instructions in previous sections of this guide apply to growing blueberry plants in containers as well as in the landscape or garden.

Getting Creative With Blueberry Plants

Plant blueberries in children's gardens
or near play structures to encourage healthy snacking.

•

Plant blueberries in patio pots
in all climates for year-round interest.

•

Give the healthy, long-lasting gift of blueberry plants.
Consider including a beautiful pot,
soil mix or other complementary items.

•

Use blueberries in large pots at weddings,
reunions, cocktail parties and other celebrations.

•

Mix blueberries with other ornamentals in pots
or in the landscape to provide four-season interest.

Simple Seasonal Care

Winter – prune
Early Spring – fertilize
Late Spring – fertilize again
Summer – harvest fruit
Fall – mulch

Blueberry Troubleshooting

Q:

Why did some of the branches on my blueberry plant die out?

A:

It's natural for branches to die out after harvest. Usually it's the top 6 inches or so, and you'll find it where the fruit was prior to harvest. Prune out this dead wood.

Q:

My blueberry plant died.

A:

The most likely causes are that the plant was too dry or over-fertilized.

Q:

I planted my blueberry plant in the wrong location.
Is it possible to transplant it?

A:

Yes. Just be sure to wait until fall or winter when the plant begins to go dormant. There may still be some green in the base of the shoots, but the tops should be dry and brittle. Follow the guidelines in this booklet under sections headed Site Selection, Soil Preparation and Planting.

Q:

I have lots of green fruit but it never seems to ripen
and then it disappears.

A:

Birds are sneaky. They keep an eye on the blueberries daily, and as soon as the fruit turns blue, they steal it! Try covering your plants with bird netting. You'll quickly see your berries ripen and can then enjoy the fruit.

Q:

Why isn't my plant growing?
It seems to stay the same size year after year.

A:

Make sure your plant(s) are grown in full sun, have soil that's amended with lots of organic matter and have adequate water. Another common reason plants don't grow is that they are over-fruited without proper pruning. If there are too many berries, all the plant's energy goes into the fruit and not to the growth of the plant. Prune your plant harder in the winter. (See pruning section.)

Q:

Why do the leaves on my plants have browned edges?

A:

There are two likely reasons for browned edges. One is not enough water. Dig in the soil and feel near the root zone. The soil should feel moist. Also, did you fertilize in the last 10 days? It could be fertilizer burn from over-fertilizing. The remedy to both issues is a slow, thorough soaking. Extreme heat can also turn leaves brown or cause the plants to lose some leaves. This shouldn't hurt the plant and the leaves will grow back if you keep the plants moist.

Q:

Some years my blueberry plant produces lots of berries; other years I get a fraction of that amount.

A:

The most likely culprit is over-fruiting on the high yield years that stunts the plant's new growth or not pruning hard enough. (See pruning section)

Q:

How can I control weeds around my blueberries?

A:

Spreading 2 to 4 inches of mulch over the roots helps prevent weed growth in addition to conserving moisture, insulating roots from cold temperatures and adding vital organic material to the soil. Use bark mulch, acid compost, sawdust or grass clippings, and repeat every other year. Be sure not to mulch with bark or sawdust from cedar or redwood. If you use grass clippings for mulch, be sure to mix with bark, pine needles or straw.
Pull any weeds that grow through the mulch before they produce seeds.

Q:

How do I know if I have soil suitable for growing blueberries?

A:

Because blueberries prefer acid soil, it's important to determine the pH of your soil to grow them successfully. Many garden centers will test a soil sample for pH level for you, or you can buy an inexpensive, easy-to-use pH test kit at most nurseries or hardware stores.
However, there's a shortcut to determining if blueberries will do well in your soil.
If you can readily grow azaleas or rhododendrons in your soil, it should be suitable for blueberries, too, since they all prefer the same acidic soil.

Q:

How long do blueberry plants last?

A:

The lifespan of blueberry plants is comparable to many fruit trees. While many factors affect their longevity, well-tended plants can live 10 or more years, making them a great investment!

Online Resource

While Fall Creek Farm & Nursery is a wholesale producer of blueberry stock for nurseries and commercial growers, we enjoy sharing our extensive knowledge with individual gardeners. For more information about growing blueberries in your home garden, please visit our website, www.fallcreeknursery.com, and click on the "Home Gardeners" tab. *We regret that we don't have staff available to respond to home gardening questions on the phone or by email. If you have more questions, please contact your local garden center or extension agents. They're the experts in your area.*

Health Benefits

Blueberries are nature's goodness. In addition to providing dietary fiber, they contain many antioxidants such as vitamin C and vitamin E. Antioxidants protect the body against some chronic diseases linked to aging. Blueberries have been known to improve memory, lower cholesterol, improve vision, prevent macular degeneration, and prevent and fight certain cancers. All this, and just 40 calories in a half cup!

Recipes

❖━━━◆◆◆━━━❖

Overnight Mini Blueberry Sweet Rolls
(*Cort and Amelie Brazelton's childhood favorite*)

Sweet rolls for two 9" pie plates

Blueberry Filling:
Mix these ingredients and set aside.
½ cup flour
¼ cup granulated sugar
¼ cup brown sugar, packed
I teaspoon cinnamon
8 tablespoons (or one cube) margarine or butter

1½ cups fresh or frozen (thawed) blueberries –
Measure into separate bowl and set aside.

Sweet Roll Dough:
3 – 3¾ cups flour
⅓ cup sugar
½ teaspoon salt
I package active dry yeast
I cup milk
¼ cup margarine or butter
I egg

In large bowl, combine 1½ cups flour, sugar, salt, and yeast. Blend well. In small sauce pan, heat milk and ¼ cup margarine until hot (120-130 degrees F). Add hot liquid and egg to flour mixture. Blend at low speed until moistened, then beat 2 minutes at medium speed. Stir in an additional 1¼ cups flour until dough pulls cleanly from the sides of the bowl. On floured surface, knead in ¼ to ½ cup flour until dough is smooth and elastic, about 5 minutes. Place in a greased bowl, cover loosely with plastic wrap and cloth towel. Let rise in warm place (80 to 85 degrees F) until doubled in size, about 45 minutes.

Grease two 9 inch round pans. Remove cover from dough and punch down dough several times to remove all air bubbles. Cut dough in half. On lightly floured surface, roll out half of the dough into a 16x6 inch rectangle. Sprinkle half of Blueberry Filling mixture evenly over dough and top with half the blueberries. Starting with 16 inch side, roll up tightly and then press seam firmly to seal. Cut long roll into 16 slices and place cut side down in one greased pan. Cover with greased plastic wrap and refrigerate overnight. (Repeat this process for each pan of sweet rolls.)

Remove pans from refrigerator and let stand at room temperature for 1 hour. Heat oven to 375 degrees F. Uncover rolls. Bake for 22 to 27 minutes or until deep golden brown. Remove from oven and serve warm. If desired, drizzle with powdered sugar glaze*.

*To make powdered sugar glaze, in small bowl combine 1 cup powdered sugar and enough water for desired drizzling consistency (about 4 to 6 teaspoons). Blend well and drizzle over warm rolls. Serve.

AUNT BEV'S BLUEBERRY MUFFIN RECIPE
(From Dave Brazelton's family's New Hampshire blueberry farm)

Cream together:
½ cup margarine
1 cup sugar
2 eggs

Then add:
2 cups flour
2 teaspoons baking powder
½ teaspoon salt
½ cup milk
1 teaspoon vanilla
2 cups blueberries (fresh or thawed frozen)

Mix together and spoon into a muffin pan. Bake for approximately 20 minutes at 375 degrees F. Makes 12 to 18 muffins.

About Fall Creek Farm & Nursery, Inc.

Fall Creek Farm & Nursery® is the world's leading wholesale blueberry nursery stock producer. From our state-of-the-art growing facilities in Oregon, Fall Creek specializes in the propagation, production and global distribution of blueberry nursery stock. We work with the leading nursery stock growers and retailers to bring you the very best that blueberries offer. We continue to develop new and exciting varieties. In the future, look for our release of new cultivars with exceptional ornamental qualities in your favorite garden centers.

Notes

....
....
....
....
....
....
....
....
....
....
....
....

Notes

....
....
....
....
....
....
....
....
....
....
....
....
....